Contents

What is Skiing?

Skiing is a means of transport using skis to glide on snow. Variations of purpose include basic transport, a recreational activity, or a competitive winter sport. Many types of competitive skiing events are recognized by the International Olympic Committee (IOC), and the International Ski Federation (FIS).

History of Skiing

Skiing has a history of almost five millennia. Although modern skiing has evolved from beginnings in Scandinavia, it may have been practiced more than 100 centuries ago in what is now China, according to an interpretation of ancient paintings. However, this continues to be debated.

The word "ski" is one of a handful of words that Norway has exported to the international community. It comes from the Old Norse word "skíð" which means "split piece of wood or firewood".

Asymmetrical skis were used in northern Finland and Sweden until at least the late 19th century. On one foot, the skier wore a long straight non-arching ski for sliding, and a shorter ski was worn on the other foot for kicking. The underside of the short ski was either plain or covered with animal skin to aid this use, while the long ski supporting the weight of the skier was treated with animal fat in a similar manner to modern ski waxing.

Early skiers used one long pole or spear. The first depiction of a skier with two ski poles dates to 1741.

Troops on continental Europe were equipped with skis by 1747.

Skiing was primarily used for transport until the mid-19th century, but since then has also become a recreation and sport. Military ski races were held in Norway during the 18th century, and ski warfare was studied in the late 18th century. As equipment evolved and ski lifts were developed during the late 19th and early 20th centuries, two main genres of skiing emerged—Alpine (downhill) skiing and Nordic skiing. The main difference between the two is the type of ski binding (the way in which the ski boots are attached to the skis).

Types of Skiing

Alpine

Also called "downhill skiing", Alpine skiing typically takes place on a piste at a ski resort. It is characterized by fixed-heel bindings that attach at both the toe and the heel of the skier's boot. Ski lifts, including chairlifts, bring skiers up the slope. Backcountry skiing can be accessed by helicopter, snowcat, hiking and snowmobile. Facilities at resorts can include night skiing, après-ski, and glade skiing under the supervision of the ski patrol and the ski school. Alpine skiing branched off from the older Nordic type of skiing around the 1920s when the advent of ski lifts meant that it was no longer necessary to climb back uphill. Alpine equipment has specialized to the point where it can now only be used with the help of lifts.

4

Nordic

The Nordic disciplines include cross-country skiing and ski jumping, which both use bindings that attach at the toes of the skier's boots but not at the heels. Cross-country skiing may be practiced on groomed trails or in undeveloped backcountry areas. Ski jumping is practiced in certain areas that are reserved exclusively for ski jumping.

Telemark

Telemark skiing is a ski turning technique and FIS-sanctioned discipline, which is named after the Telemark region of Norway. It uses equipment similar to Nordic skiing, where the ski bindings are attached only at the toes of the ski boots, allowing the skier's heel to be raised throughout the turn. However, the skis themselves are often the same width as Alpine skis.

Equipments

Equipment used in skiing includes:

- Skis, which may have skins applied or be textured for uphill traction or wax applied for minimizing sliding friction. Twin-tip skis are designed to move forwards or backwards.
- Boots and bindings
- Poles
- Helmets
- Ski suits
- Ski goggles
- Skiing gloves

Top Tips for First-Time Skiers

1. Pack warm and waterproof clothing

The challenge begins before you even strap into your skis...with your clothes! It's incredibly important to pack thick, waterproof outerwear (pants and a coat), as well as thermal base layers and wool socks for underneath your coats. The outerwear will keep water and snow out, while the thermal layer will wick sweat and keep you extra warm.

For outerwear, we strongly recommend purchasing high quality outdoor wear from brands like Columbia, Burton, or Helly Hansen. A good ski set is waterproof and insulated, with lots of pockets to put your important stuff.

Thermal wear comes in lots of fabrics and varieties, but there is no better sweat-wicking cloth than Merino wool. Warm and dry yet lightweight and cozy, Merino wool base layers are the perfect pair for thick outerwear.

2. Wear goggles & a helmet

Not only do you need adequate clothing, but goggles and a helmet are a must for safety and protection. Goggles will help you keep flying snow out of your eyes, which can be especially problematic on snowy days or when there's artificial snow being blown. Additionally, many sets of ski goggles are UV resistant as well, protecting your eyes from the harsh rays of the sun.

Additionally, a helmet is an important piece of gear to wear on the slopes. While you can purchase your own helmet, many ski resorts do have them for rent along with their other gear. Be sure to do your own research to make sure you have a helmet available!

3. Take a Backpack

The weather changes in the mountains, all the time. To familiarise yourself with its many moods, keep an eye on our snow report, as well as checking out webcams in your chosen resort from time to time.

That way, you'll avoid the usual mistake of dressing for the weather you wake up to, and nothing else. Yes, it may be a pleasant +3C in the sunshine when you leave the chalet, but if the cloud comes down and the wind picks up it could be -13C in an instant. It works the other way too: you dress for a blizzard, the sun come out, and you sweat out what feels like half your body weight.

The only way to cope with the changes, is to carry a backpack. Always pack spare clothing (unless you are wearing it all), as well as something to drink. You can of course carry your lunch too – and save yourself a fortune in the mountain restaurants.

If you don't already have a good backpack, Snow+Rock and Ellis Brigham have all the top brands, from Camelbak to Black Diamond. When you buy, make sure your pack has a waistband, and strap at chest height that connects the two shoulder straps. You'll need these to stop the pack from flapping about when you get more active.

4. Choose a beginner-friendly ski resort

While most ski resorts do have options for beginners, not all are created equal when it comes to first-time skiers. The good news is you can find beginner-friendly ski resorts practically all around the world.

There are lots of specific characteristics of a ski resort that can contribute to a good learning environment for less experienced skiers. While not comprehensive, a beginner-friendly ski resort will have the following characteristics at a minimum:

- Gear rentals

- Ski lessons (group or private)

- Bunny hills and beginner-friendly "green" trails

More on each of these later, but for now, you can start your research with these items in mind to choose a destination that accommodates first-time skiers.

5. Rent your larger equipment

You may be tempted to drop a ton of money on your own skis and boots, but we'd recommend holding off on this until you've got some experience under your belt. Not only is transporting ski equipment incredibly difficult, but it's also very expensive.

Instead of buying skis, you can usually rent them from any ski resort for a reasonable fee. Renting allows you to get a feel for skis and get fit advice from an expert. Employees at basically every ski resort can take your measurements and make sure you're fully outfitted for your first time out in the snow.

Once you're more experienced, you can consider buying your own skis, but for your first few time, we recommend saving yourself some money and renting everything.

6. Take an introductory lesson

Taking a group or individual ski lesson is a great way to learn the basics of skiing in a supportive, hands-on way. Ski instructors are trained to teach absolute beginners and will help you learn the motions and techniques needed to become a more seasoned skier.

Luckily, most ski resorts offer lessons that range from first-time skiers to advanced. If you've never been skiing before or it's been several years, a group lesson is a fantastic, cost-effective way to learn the ropes.

17

We recommend looking for resorts that offer a few different levels of classes, and that separate adults and children in group lessons. If you've got a few days at the resort, it could also be a good idea to take a few classes to sharpen your skills and get expert help with your technique.

7. Forget the poles (for now)

You've probably seen photos of skiers barreling down slopes with skiing poles in hand. However, for your first few times out in the slopes, you probably won't need poles (and your instructor(s) will probably tell you to leave them behind).

Why? Because they'll most likely get in your way as you're learning.

Of course, take the recommendation of your ski instructor or the gear rental folks, but most beginner lessons will advise you to leave the poles behind.

8. Opt for an all-in-one package

Pro tip: if you're new to snow sports, you can often save big on the costs of skiing for beginners. For first-time skiers, many resorts offer packages at a pretty hefty discount that include ski rentals, lessons, and lift tickets.

Often, these packages cost even less if you buy multiple days in a row. Sometimes, these discounts can constitute savings of 25-50% off the full price of rentals, lift tickets, and lessons all-in. If you're planning a skiing weekend getaway, do some research to see if your resort offers a discount for newbies.

9. Bend your knees

It can feel natural to get nervous and stiff up or lock your knees when you're skiing for the first time. However, this will usually just cause you to lose your balance!

Instead, as you're skiing down the slopes, keep your knees bent and flexible so you can go over bumps and around curves with more fluidity and ease. The more you allow your knees to bend and move, the easier it will be to navigate through the snow (and the less likely you'll be to go out of control or fall!).

10. Embrace the "pizza" formation

When you take your lessons, you'll probably learn the "pizza" formation of aligning your skis. Expert skiers you see on TV or out on the slopes will have their skis parallel to each other, but when you're first starting out, you'll want to keep your toes slightly pointed inward to make sure you aren't going too fast or skiing out of control.

The pizza formation is not only the way to control your speed, but it's also a way to stop completely. Learning how to stop on your skis is an essential skill that you should truly aim to master, as stopping gives you the ultimate level of control over your velocity and movements. Practicing and owning the pizza formation, both while moving and when stopping, is an important skill that you'll use throughout your skiing journey.

11. Look up, not down

This one might seem self-explanatory, but when you're out on the ski trails, it can be easy to break. While you're skiing down the slopes, be sure to keep your eyes ahead of you, NOT on your feet. Keep your gaze centered down the hill to your destination and keep your eyes ahead, otherwise you could easily lose your balance or run into someone in front of you.

Looking ahead is not only helpful for balance, but it's also necessary for your safety and protection.

12. Start out on smooth, easy slopes

After you've got a few runs under your belt, you probably feel ready for the double black diamond trails…right? *Probably not.*

Our suggestion is to stick to easy trails (green trails and training areas) for the first several times you're skiing, so you can practice proper techniques like turning and stopping. The more you practice on easy trails, the less you'll have to worry about things like jumps, drops, and obstacles in your way. It's safer to stick to easier trails when you're starting out.

Once you feel totally confident in your skills (over several days of skiing), you can try some of the next-level blue trails. Don't worry, they can wait for you!

13. Don't be afraid of falling

Spoiler alert: you're undoubtedly going to fall when you're learning how to ski. It's inevitable. You might fall on your side, or faceplant, or get your legs tangled in all kinds of impossible ways. You might not even know how you fell. However, what's most important is that you pick yourself up and remain confident as you continue to learn and practice your skills.

Why? Because everyone, *everyone* falls when they're learning to ski. So, don't fear it. Embrace it.

14. Take lots of breaks & hydrate often

It has been 4 hours, you've been zipping down the slopes like a pro…and you're exhausted. Don't forget to take breaks to rest and, most importantly, continue to hydrate. Because it's cold and snowy, it can be easy to forget to take breaks and drink water, but this is an absolute must, especially because skiing is such a workout!

When we go skiing, we always bring a Hydro Flask with ice water inside so we always have access to ice cold, clean water between ski runs. However you choose to handle your breaks, be sure to take them often and with plenty of water on the side!

15. Learn to control your speed

When you're learning to ski, going fast is easy…but going slowly is not. In addition to flying down the slopes at top speed, make time to practice control and speed regulation. Your instructors should teach you some strategies for this, like skiing in curves and using the "pizza" formation, but employing these skills on the big slopes is really the only way to improve your control on the trails.

Getting a feel for different speeds and mechanisms for control is a critical part of any skier's journey, and it's good to keep those skills sharp as you transition from a novice to a more experienced skier.

16. Practice makes perfect (so just keep doing it!)

You're going to fall, you're going to get tired, and you're going to get snow down your pants. We've all been there. But one of the best things about skiing is that there's always something new to learn, practice, and perfect.

No matter what level of skier you are, we challenge you to get out there and learn new skills. Take the time to practice, practice, practice. And continue to enjoy the journey and thrill of our favorite winter sport. There are tons of resources on skiing for beginners (including on this site!), but the only way to truly learn is by getting out there, strapping in your skis, and hitting the trails.

The Essential Biomechanics of Skiing

Positioning

When you are skiing you will find your position changes all the time. For beginners, the key thing to focus on is having your knees bent and legs parallel. Another option is to have your legs ready in a snow plow position, with the tips of your skis almost together. The bent knees are there to help you absorb any bumps and moguls you may ski over.

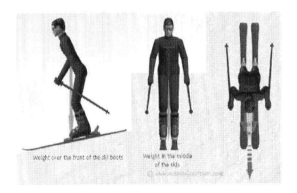

Weight over the front of the ski boots   Weight in the middle of the skis

Stance

You will need to be leaning into the skins of your ski boots. This will improve your balance and control as you ski on all the slope terrain. Picture yourself ready to dive into a swimming pool. You lean forward not back. You need to always be ready to set off.

Flex & Gaze

Your entire body must be ready for action. Besides bent knees, have your elbows bent at an angle of roughly 75 degrees in front of you. This will allow your poles to fall into the correct position on their own. With your body weight central on your skis, look straight in front of you. You need to always see the slope in front, not your feet!

Correct Use of Poles

Hands Positioning

With your arms at either side holding your poles, lift your forearms so they are in front of you. Aim for an angle of around 70-80 degrees (shy of a right angle). Keeping your poles in front of you in this way will shift your body weight forward. This subtle change will improve your control of your skis as your toes near the tip of your ski boots.

Only Subtle Wrist Movement

If you are holding your poles correct, you will only need to move your wrist when skiing. If you start waving your arms around, you will lose balance. Practice the motion of planting your poles only moving your wrists several times. It should look like you are 'walking your skis'. Soon this will be a natural movement and you will find it easier to use your poles in more advanced maneuvers.

Lock torso

Keep your torso in the direction it is going. A common mistake is to twist your body when skiing downhill. Doing this will put your arms in the wrong place. You will lose balance and control, struggling to regain the correct stance.

The First Things To Practice

Learn how to stop

This should always be the first thing you master. Once you can start and stop safely on skis you won't endanger yourself or anyone else on the slope. Don't attempt any busy or hard runs until you have learned this skill.

Don't go fast

A common phrase in younger skiers is 'just bomb it'. When you haven't learned good control of your skis, make sure you go at your own pace. Take your time and increase your speed over time. Avoid going home in an ambulance on your first day!

Round off turns

Don't be afraid to complete your wide turns. It takes practice to narrow these turns and be able to complete short turns downhill. This is a great way to keep your speed under control. If you find yourself unable to slow down when finishing a turn, you likely didn't complete the one prior.

Slowly progress to parallel

You will find the more you ski in a snow plow, the more your body will position your feet in a more parallel stance. When you feel your feet wanting to progress to parallel, then learn this step. Don't attempt it before you have full control of your skis.

Warm down techniques

As important as it is too warm up, it is important to warm down. During skiing, your body will use a lot of physicalities. Without taking the time to release some tension after a ski session, you will risk gaining sore limbs. These sore muscles will interfere with your ability to enjoy your following ski days. The Warren Smith Ski Academy also created a useful tutorial on how to stretch after a ski.

Know how to fall

The key to keeping your injuries to a minimum is to spread out the impact area. Avoid landing on singular limbs. A larger surface area will absorb more of your fall.

Know how to get up

Whether your skis are still on off will not matter. When you have fallen, you need to position your skis, parallel across the slope (not downhill). Next, dig your poles in behind you to counter your balance as you push up into a standing position. From here you can ski off into a new turn with ease.

Know how to get your skis back on

When you lose a ski in the powder, it can be a nightmare for beginners to get it back on. The trick is to put on your downhill ski first. Once this is on, it is much easier to stand into your uphill ski. Remember to kick off any excess snow from your ski boot, and you won't have any trouble getting your bindings on.

Where to practice

Slopeside

This will always be the best place to practice your skiing. You can't beat learning on an actual mountain. The terrain and conditions will reflect what you will face when you skiing on your own or with friends.

Indoor Slope

These are starting to become more popular worldwide. Indoor 'real snow' slopes are a great substitute for the mountain if you live far away from resorts. Or if you want to stay in form during the summer, these indoor slopes will help you keep your ski game!

Dry slope

These outdoor slopes are usually made of neveplast or snowflex materials. They replicate the texture and feel of snow. Dry slopes are a great way to practice all year round regardless of the weather.

Airbags

When you are new learning tricks for the park safety should always first. If you have access to a foam pit or air bag on your slopes, this is a great way to practice. Once you are landing the tricks well, take them to the park for real.

Trampolines

If you are learning spins and flips, trampolining is a good way to practice. You can master your rotation so you can 'feel' the correct speed before trying them on the snow. Most centers will also have a foam pit or airbag for big tricks too. Make the most of these and then progress to a slope-side airbag before showing off your skills at the park.

Printed in Great Britain
by Amazon

75750834R00031